ABRAH and JESUS Begin...

25
Messages from Heaven

CHANNELLED BY OLIVIA & RAF OCAÑA

First published by Ocaña Consulting Publishing 2018.

Channelled and written by Olivia & Raf Ocaña

Cover design and formatting by Helen Poole

To find out more about The Law of Attraction and Abraham-Hicks, © by Jerry & Esther Hicks please visit www.AbrahamHicks.com

ISBN 978-1-9164029-0-4

We dedicate this book to those that seek love and seek joy and seek guidance in their lives. We have given these words to Raf and Olivia to present to those of you that are drawn to this book, that we love and cherish and that seek our help.

Read these words with an open heart and believe that they can make a difference to you and they will, we can assure you of that.

Our blessings to all.

Abraham and Christ Collective Consciousnesses

CONTENTS

ABOUT THE AUTHORS

RAF

My story is no more remarkable than anyone else's. I have had a life full of ups and downs as have we all. The loss of my brother at a young age took its toll on me and left me with more limiting beliefs about myself and those around me than I realised. For years I struggled with the loss, buried deeply within me and stopping the real me from appearing.

This loss always gave me a true sense of spirituality especially when my brother who had passed came to me when I was a teenager. This visit from him cemented a belief in me that there was a life after death for us, and that belief gave me so much strength throughout many other difficult times in my life, to know that he was there with me in some way was both comforting and strength giving.

I was not one of these people that 'had a gift' as it were, and my life until my early forties continued in a very normal way, full of the joys of friends and family and of course the tough times mixed in with that along the way. I was always quite sensitive emotionally and until recently thought that many of these emotions were my own, when in fact I now know that they were often those of others that I was picking up on and at times absorbing.

Something changed for me in my forties and my spiritual growth was literally forced upon me and yet I still denied it, unaware of its existence and putting many of the ailments that came as a result of it down to ill health and stress. It wasn't until I received a reading from a spiritual medium one day that she explained everything I was experiencing, all these health problems, the anxiety, the low vibrational moments were down to spirit, desperately wanting to talk to me.

What followed was a period where I tried to open up to this but no matter what I tried to do, nothing happened, I had assumed that the medium was wrong and I went about my life as before, managing the health problems and trying my best to enjoy life. But something was missing, not quite right with me and no matter how hard I tried I couldn't escape the trauma that at times I was now feeling.

There was nothing I could put these very negative strong

emotions down to and despite living in a wonderful home with an amazing wife and family and circle of friends I continued to spiral. Something had to change, I knew this, I was acting out of character, and at times tried to lose myself in a few drinks or a night out just to rid myself of these awful feelings I was experiencing; but this couldn't go on.

It was at this time that my wife Olivia started to see changes in herself and her gift to heal. It was this amazing discovery of hers that opened the door for me to heal myself. There was no coincidence to this, and very soon her amazing gifts allowed me to lift the fog that had been surrounding me for literally years. My emotional, mental and even physical wellbeing was transformed, and with this transformation came the headspace for me to really tackle what was happening to me.

Channelling the messages in this book, at times have been like writing an auto-biography for me. The changes I had been able to make to my personal wellbeing prior to receiving the words written here gave me the platform to move towards what is was that was calling me. And with that came a renewed passion, belief and desire in my life, something that had long been drained from me.

A reading from another medium once again confirmed my spiritual gifts, and in her words a 'very strong one'.

She encouraged me to join her spiritual development course as this she believed could help me protect myself from the spiritual energies that were still so weighing down my own energy. I went into this course with only the removal of those energies in mind but what was to happen I could never have imagined.

It was like an explosion and within only a few months I had discovered the ability to receive messages from non-physical energies in so many ways. Things started with images in my mind's eye, then words channelled, the receiving of psychic drawings, the ability to voice channel many different non-physical energies, and today discussions with spirit can be like a conversation with a person sat next to me, so clear are the thoughts that they give me as they speak to me.

This brings me to the spirits and guides that I now am lucky enough to receive. All of them fill my life now with such devotion and love for me, their support and encouragement is truly life giving emotionally and they have made such difference to who I am. This is not to say that they have changed me in any way, merely that they have allowed the inner me, my true Self to come out and blend with the person that I have always been to those that know me.

My team is one of the highest order and I say this not to place any importance on myself, this is not something I am at all comfortable with in many ways. However these guides, friends, in the spiritual world are taking me on a path that I could never have dreamed of. I don't exactly know where this is leading me, all I do know is that I have total faith in them and working with them has been one of the most wonderful experiences of my life.

This book highlights two of these guides that have been working with me and no doubt over time the other wonderful non-physical Beings that are also with me at the moment, will bring something else wonderful to you all. For this I do know, they have not come to me merely to help me find myself in a better place, they so wish to share their love and more importantly, their insight with anyone that wishes to hear it. How this will happen I do not know but I cannot wait to find out.

For now, I say only that I hope the messages in this book bring you a small piece of comfort or inspiration. No doubt these words will raise many questions and it is clear to me that Jesus and Abraham will want to make themselves available to answer them.

OLIVIA

The age I am writing this now, I'm 41 and it's fair to say I have lived a life so far full of plenty of adventure, self-exploration, challenges and total joy and happiness. I was born into a dramatic situation, where through a random act of violence, my darling father was taken from us all and just 5 days before I was born. As you can imagine, the impact of this one act caused a ripple effect through not only my beautiful Mother and me the unborn, but the entire family; one that would continue to make waves to this present day.

With that as a backdrop, I was known as the ray of sunshine, the light in the darkness. I had an incredible childhood, my Mother, Grandfather, Brother, Aunty and other family members ensured that this was the case. My Mother is incredibly spiritual, gentle and kind and taught me a lot about the depth of the human soul, inner strength, the ability to trust your instincts and the wonder of kindness.

I had a few troubled times, but they really passed quite quickly, and on the whole, I was incredibly happy, driven, focused, with some talents – although not really in anything in particular. My ability to heal wasn't something that was known then to me. I had, on many occasions, people say that I just made them feel better, that I was wise beyond my years, I always knew the right thing to say…that kind of thing. I never thought myself as 'gifted', in fact that was something that I always attributed to my other family members. I wasn't to be one of the lucky ones, so to speak.

I was a natural manifester, I found that anything that I wanted, truly wanted I was able to manifest. I had a huge sense of 'knowing' about things, and was able to read situations easily, was able to diffuse confrontation, was often able to help others, at work I was known as 'the fixer'. I made stuff happen when I really wanted it to. I also was able to cram in a crazy amount all day every day without getting hugely effected, I recall so many people would say, 'I don't know how she does it!'

It was in my late thirties after years in a Corporate job, and after a couple of failed entrepreneurial attempts, I had the husband and the children I had always wanted (my beautiful children, all three of them) and the house that I had dreamt of, but I started to feel like there was always something more meant for me but I couldn't put my finger on it. I started to think about retraining as a surgeon or a clinical scientist. This yearning for more led me on a huge path of spiritual growth but it was stop/start (mainly stopping!) until September 2017. This coincided with my 'awakening'.

After listening to my own inner guidance, and what it was I was really meant to be doing, following the signs, the breadcrumbs on my path – I got it. I started to heal my own gorgeous husband who I would do anything for, and finally I could help him. I learned more about myself and my own spiritual connection and 'gifts' than anyone could ever teach me or explain by literally being full of faith, trust and belief, by following my own instincts, by understanding the smallest results, by tuning in and receiving. This totally coincided with Raf's own expansion and luckily for us, it happened, just as it was meant to, completely side by side.

I have now learned that I am able to amplify peoples own connection to their Source energy, that is my unique gift and purpose in this world. The energy practices that I am given are all about cellular change, direction and influence but it is your own energy that is used to heal. These Energy Practices are given to me by 'The Team' of which Abraham and Jesus (the Collectives) are a part of, but there are a number of other entities, Archangels and Collectives that also form part of 'The Team'. Abraham has always been with me, and Abraham is my main guide, my main teacher and is my ultimate gateway to 'The Team' and whom I channel.

Through this expansion, I have been given many gifts now that provide the ability to 'read' people cellularly, and I am given cellular activation techniques, routes through the body, I even see organs and body systems almost 3D in my mind's eye. I believe that many more abilities are coming and as I continue on this path, my gifts are getting stronger and stronger, and I know more will be provided. I have helped hundreds of people all over the world and will continue to do so with as many people and as often as I can.

If you had asked me even a year ago whether this was what I could see in my future, the answer would have been no. It has been the most incredible expansion and beyond my wildest dreams. I have to thank my darling Raf as he has been with me, stuck by my side and together, we have done this. Without him, I probably would have slowed it down or disbelieved or even stopped altogether for a while, but the two of us together, just as was always meant to be, means that here we are in front of the world, delivering new messages from Abraham and Jesus.

I am honoured, I am beyond grateful and appreciative of all I have been given. I sometimes pinch myself and wonder if it is all a dream, but this is now our reality and our future. I wish that for anyone reading this, who wonders if such a thing is possible for them, to start from the smallest feeling of 'rightness' within you and move from that place. This can lead you to wonderful insight, connection and magic. True magic exists for us on earth, it is however within us first and always.

INTRODUCTION

You are everything to us. This is something we wish for you to know. You are treasured, loved, supported, honoured and we are forever grateful to you, for it is you – here, now, in this life, in this physical experience who is determining the growth and expansion of all Universal energy. You are this important.

We have come together as two Collective Consciousnesses to bring you new words for this time. We see the good, we see the expansion and the growth of all and now is the time for us to support you in a new way, a way that will help you heal, help you open your eyes to new understanding and help you let go of things that are no longer serving you.

Who are we? We are Abraham and Jesus. Known by many, beloved by many but we are Collectives. This means that we are not one but many. We are no single soul, no single life entity but we are a collection of consciousness. For Jesus, this represents the Christ Consciousness energy and not specifically Jesus Christ, the soul of Jesus is of course part of this consciousness, but the Christ Consciousness energy transcends any religious or political alignment and brings a message that is for all people regardless of their beliefs or who they are. Abraham is the much beloved Abraham that is the teacher of The Law of Attraction that Esther and Jerry Hicks have made their life's work. Abraham too is a collective consciousness formed of teachers and is able to provide clarity and insight to all on all things. The blending of the two, this is what will inspire, what will provide you the clarity you seek, the reminder of all that you know somewhere deep inside you.

We work with Olivia and Raf as they are clear channels for us, this means that we are able to speak, write and work through them, they translate us vibrationally, this is something that is possible for many but they are chosen specifically for this, for us, for this time. They are beloved to us, by us but so are you all. We are grateful for them to be able to bring these words to you. They are unique in their experience, this has taken longer than you will know to provide this ability but it is all perfect timing, perfectly aligned in motion and always as it was meant to be.

There will be many more books, many more subjects,

many more offerings from us. This is our first book for the world at this time. We have asked Olivia and Raf to own these words on our behalf, but know that they are for each and every one of you. To feel, to know, to understand and to release any past confusion, doubt and fear that you may have had. This is the truth. When you read these words they will resonate somewhere deeply inside of you. You will remember, you will feel this to be true. And so it is and always will be.

We love you.

Abraham and Jesus.

MESSAGE 1

WHO AM I?

If only you knew. Knew how you chose this life, this very existence. How eagerly you awaited the ability to be on earth, the anticipation was great. For life on earth is the greatest ability for collective growth and you, you are one of the luckiest for you are here now, in this unchartered territory.

There has never before been this very moment in time, nor the next. You are literally at the leading edge of thought. The realness of this life, the ability to learn and understand, to challenge and progress. Your ability to choose. Your total freedom to choose. All for a purpose. No matter what, it is all for the greatest good. There are no victors nor losers, it is all equal at the start, during and at the end and beyond. Every single life matters. Every single moment matters, the good, the bad, the ugly, the magnificent, for it all leads to something. That something is the continued evolution of our Universe, our God loving Universe. For when there is darkness, you seek light. For when there is love, you wish to give love. When there is abundance, you wish to share it. Where there is knowledge, you still want to learn more.

We are all energy, we are all connected. You are Universal, this is true. You belong to the Universe, this is also true. What you do, think and feel all impacts the Universe. You are that special. You are that divine. Each person carries their divinity. This diverse world is full of the divine. Every single person.

You have a Soul Contract for this life. It is not a solemn occasion when defined, but it is held in very high regard, with the greatest importance. There are certain things that you are meant to do. This defines your purpose. This does not map out every single nuance, every twist and turn, every meeting and missed or gained opportunity, nor is it time-bound. You do not have a duty to find it and honour it but you feel differently if you don't when you are living your life. This is your cue to wake up, to remember as it is to your very soul, your very core, the essence of you, your Inner Being that your Soul Contract resides. You know inside yourself if you are doing what you are 'meant' to be doing. You definitely know when you aren't, because you feel that disconnect, that dissatisfaction with life, that itch that you can't scratch. This is why it is there, why you can't seem to shake it off. No matter what you do to distract yourself, your Inner Being is calling you. You can ignore it. You can literally choose anything you like, you have total and utter free will.

Not only do you have your Inner Being completely on your side, with you always and always wanting the best for you as the sacred holder of your soul contract – you have us. When we say us, we mean the non-physical energy; the energy that creates worlds, we are all the same, we are Godforce, we are Archangels, we are Soul Collectives, Collective Consciousness, we are ancestral guides, we are entities and spirit guides and almighty. We are here to gently remind you of who you are and what you are here to do. We are here to nudge you, to protect you, to be here if you ever call. To answer you when you ask. You may not yet be open to the answer from us, you may not even feel that we have responded, but we always have.

You know who you are. You know your life's purpose. It is within you always. Do not fear it. Do not get frustrated in the finding of it. Recognise it is feeling that will help you remember. You need to become re-tuned to your Inner Being. You need to notice when you are on or off your path. If it has been some time since you have truly been happy, recognise that this is just because you are not living the life you are meant to. This can be remedied but it takes commitment and focus. This is not something you can get a quick fix for, but once you start you will notice the difference and quickly. Step by step, bit by bit you will feel better, you will feel that fire, that excitement again, that knowing of all you are.

MESSAGE 2

THE SELF

Be it a feeling that comes from within or from another, the Self is not an easy thing to take care of in this world today. Nevertheless, we strongly advise you to recognise within you the power that the Self can achieve. What is meant by the Self? This is your one true being, your Inner Being, or your connection to Source as it is also known.

Bring the Self within you to those places that help you to recognise in you a simpler part of your soul, a place within that you have always known but perhaps have never taken the time to get to know well enough. For this is the greatest relationship that you can ever have. This relationship will always love you, believe in you and support you in your passions and your growth activities for it knows only to see you in the best possible light and does not understand why you yourself choose to see you in any other way. When we say 'you yourself' we mean all of those parts of you that make up your soul, your emotions, your ego, your mind, your physical existence and body, all make up yourself and the way in which you see your Self. There is not a difference between the Self and yourself except in your mind, body and emotional bodies and how you choose to see it. For in time if you give yourself love and give your Self love there is in fact no difference. Confusing as this may seem this is why we say to you travel within your various bodies, study your emotions, love your physicality and enjoy the ride for all of your hopes and dreams for life are connected to these elements of you.

Carry within you a torch for your Self and the bodies of the Self and rejoice in the meaningful relationship that you can have with it. Find new ways to enjoy each moment and the Self will bring you ten times that joy for you are releasing within you your very core, your very soul and to this end we say to you the beginning of your life today starts at this very understanding, and when a person brings this understanding upon their Self and all that encompasses it this person spearheads a relationship with God and the Universe. Fear not what we say here for this in itself is far simpler than you imagine. Wellbeing is your guide to the Self and wellbeing is your ultimate target and goal to achieve in cleansing and purifying and loving and preparing the Self for your precious life.

Channel all your energies into becoming the very Self that you desire, trust in what you feel when you do this. Day by day, little by little the world around you will change and what you feel as a result will be heaven within you. Love shining through from every place in your Being this is what we say to you and this comes easily if you believe it will. Generate all the love in the world for your Self and see how this love transmits itself to every part of your life in turn. Grab onto this love for dear life for this is your steed, your chariot, your path to a beautiful existence.

Take care of your sensitivity around all that causes you pain. Love it just as much as those things that bring you peace and harmony. Create a place in your life for those things that distress you or sadden you and then let them be, let them speak, let them create, for in doing so you allow them their voice and this in turn allows you to feel its pain, your consequential pain. Do not analyse too much but merely allow the Self to acknowledge it, and in time its power over you will diminish. Its need to take from you will be replaced by its acknowledgement of your love and understanding of its existence, and when this time comes my dear friend, when this time comes this is when you can let it go. Its power no longer holding you or your soul and therefore with love you release it.

So what to do when this happens? Well this leaves you with a space in your heart that can be filled with whatever you choose, whatever fills your soul with joy and then and only then can you truly allow the Self to exist as it wishes to exist. Allow this to happen to your very Being for everything that troubles you in your life as well as all that brings you joy, and you have truly found the path to a better life, and simpler life, and whole life, and a loving life. This message is one of hope and laughter and sunshine and your Self lies at the very centre of it.

MESSAGE 3

EASE

Ease is not something which, common to its meaning, comes easily to many in a world fraught with responsibility and terrors and darkness of some kind or another. However, there are those that see beyond these powerful and emotive things and in turn choose to see the world as a completely different place. The cynics of our world will reference history and facts and choose only to accept what they think they know to be true rather than what they feel. But those who choose to feel their way through life will always find a different angle on the life they lead and in doing so will forever see their world as a place of ease.

Ease can be separated into two understandings for this message. Firstly, that in which eases the mind and the soul, the Self, and secondly that in which eases the place in which we live, our surroundings, the people we love and know, and the places in which we congregate.

Ease of the mind and the soul takes little understanding of anything other than what is a feeling or a sensation that we experience at any point in time, however as has been discussed this is not always a place people wish to accept or acknowledge due to their prejudices or previous experiences. Bringing the soul to a place of ease is really a matter for the individual to accept. In doing so life becomes a better place to be and in doing so our second point comes into play, that of the world around us and the ease at which it plays with us and our Self.

There may come a time when the vibration of the earth transcends to a place where no darkness exists, that is to say earth will ascend to a place of high vibrational frequencies and Beings who have nothing but love and acceptance of each other. However, this time does not exist today and therefore it is down to the individuals upon earth to ascend within themselves and in doing so take their own small piece of the earth into their hearts and make it their reality, physically and emotionally. One can only achieve this on the premise that we have accepted that there is in fact a need to create ease in our world. The changing faces of the society in which we live at times makes it hard for us to change, for change is seen as weird or unexpected or contrary to what is understood about a person.

But for those brave enough to look at their worlds and actually take the steps to change without fear of judgement or question or comparison against themselves or indeed others, lies a pathway to God and the kingdom of heaven as it is also known. Trace the time of your forefathers and see how their worlds came to be, trace times of peace or struggle or war and understand what lead to these times and at its very core is the strength of the feeling of ease in the world and the people within it.

Understand this now, today and you too can see what influence you will have on your world and the world of others, and this my friend is the quest we place in front of you, this is the challenge that you have the gift to both write and to answer.

MESSAGE 4

MOTHER EARTH

Mother Earth is something that we use as a term of endearment for the planet in which you live but how many of you actually believe that this planet really sees you as her own children, to be nurtured and cared for. And how many of you actually realise that mother earth loves all Beings; creatures and plant life and trees in the same way as she does people? In fact every single thing on this earth belongs to her and she sees you all as her children. Some have spoken of theories with Gaia and the fact that this planet consciously works through every thing that has ever occurred on her. Let it be said that mother earth feels, breathes, senses, hurts, explores in a way that the human mind cannot comprehend and perhaps never will, but this must not detract from the fact that she is a living organism with so much to give and so much to be protected.

All life on earth is connected, all things all animals all matter, connected to each other and as such we must recognise that by taking from the planet we only steal from ourselves as human beings and this in the long run will only hurt us in the same way as we hurt what it is that we steal from in the first place.

And so why do we seek to destroy parts and elements of this beautiful world armed with this knowledge? Ask yourself this question next time you turn on a light or burn coal, and whilst there is so much of this that needs to be done for your survival ask yourself if there is anything that you could do. Think what small things you yourself can influence, what you yourself need and wish to change and see done differently, and then seek out those that can support you in delivering that change, no matter how large or small its effect on the planet. Give your future generations a platform on which to build a new planet, one that is respectful of all that is within it and all that uses her.

For we shall seek out opportunities to evolve this world once we are able to respect her and all her children on earth, land, sea and sky. Take no prisoners when it comes to the future of this planet's wellbeing and remember that she loves you and wishes only good things for you. Remember this and all will be as was meant to be, failure is not an option for this wondrous planet. Give unto her what it is that she desires just as you would your own children. Take care of her and you shall reap the rewards of a planet full of joy and light and life.

MESSAGE 5

LOVE

Love thy neighbour has never been so important a statement as it is today for we need to recognise the good that comes from such a simple statement. We hear of so much hurt and damage in this world being done by people to each other in so many different ways, and on so many different scales large and small, all of which bringing a sense of discord between those people that are interrelating. Some of us choose to recognise that our own lives are far more satisfying when we take an approach that looks to be at peace and harmony with those around us, be it a work colleague, a family member, friend or perhaps a more formal relationship at a senior leadership level within a country. All of these relationships can be approached in so many different ways but isn't it just so simple to take the view that if we approach the situation with love in all instances that we can always look to find common ground and understanding.

Our own lives are so much more enhanced when we step on the gas of love and let it escape from our every pore, our every part of us and carry it with us throughout our day. We ask not that you walk around in a permanent state of happiness for this is not possible or reality. But be kind on yourself in the first instance and with that will come a level of compassion in your heart that will express itself through all of your relationships with people.

Those of us that are lucky enough to live in our own world safely and comfortably without the worry of a roof over our head or food on the table must consider this situation one of great importance, for it is these people that have it within their gift to ultimately share their love with those less fortunate than themselves. We are not asking that you now add an additional task or job to your life where you now need to become a charitable foundation at every step of your day but only that you stop every once in a while and ask yourself can I do more to help this person here on the street or on the news on in the newspaper. This in itself is something that we can all consider in the passing of our life and would make such a difference to those who are a little less fortunate.

Leaders of our planet need to take this request a step further and seek to build on the generosity of its people and look for ways to eradicate situations where people are fleeing their homes and their families in the name of war or famine or poverty. Leaders have a chance to really make a difference and we plead with you to see this request as an opportunity to bring yourself greatness, to leave behind a legacy on the world and to truly do something amazing in your lives. For this alone will bring such peace and harmony to the planet that we treasure so dearly and for this you will be forever remembered.

MESSAGE 6

HOPE

Hope is a wonderful thing for it brings with it a myriad of emotions in the lives of those it seeks to influence. Imagine if you will, the child sitting on the edge of a wall at the end of their street longing for a little dog to walk by so that he or she can stroke him and pet him and perhaps take him home. This feeling of anticipation and of joy at the mere thought of having the opportunity to do this will give this young child a feeling within him or her that simply cannot be bought if made to come true. For this my friends is the feeling that all of us must bring to our hearts in order to bring about a joyous existence.

It is hope that gets us all out of bed and bounding towards a thought or a task and our hearts racing at the very idea of what might be. Think of hope as your antidote to the daily stresses and tasks that you fill your lives with at times. Give yourself a dose of hope every now and again and perhaps you will see your own mind take this medicine and make it its own for good. In other words, practice this as often as you can and soon it may become a permanent state of Being for you.

What could be achieved in these circumstances one can only dream of but we wish for all of you to do this today, start to hope that in some small way your life will improve, your situations will change your wellbeing will grow to new heights and your general state of mind will be opened in such wondrous and interesting ways. Your lives will now become that dream that you jumped so quickly out of bed for, and all will be well with you and just as importantly, that feeling in your world, your planet, will match your own world within your heart and your soul.

Take this small request with you wherever you go today and see how you start to feel differently throughout your life and throughout all of your experiences. For it is hope that can bring you this and it is hope that must prevail in this wondrous and glorious planet of yours.

MESSAGE 7

FAMILY

No doubt one of the emotions that one can bring to oneself is when we speak of our family. For it is family which bonds us in a way that no other thing can. There are of course some families stronger than others but at its very core the family unit holds a bond which protects, loves and expresses much of what has been spoken of so far in our messages to you. Hopes, fears, love, passion all ooze from a family at one time or another and it is these emotions that lead us all to a better place.

Your family may know little of how much you feel about them or perhaps they are aware that they are your everything, it matters not as much for all that really is important is that the feelings are there within your own heart because those feelings invoke a sense of belonging for you. This belonging is what drives you on to be a better man or woman, husband or wife, son or daughter and it is this belonging which ultimately will see you succeed. For mankind as a whole, needs this sense of family in order to grow and flourish in this world and to take on all that comes to it.

These words may seem obvious but consider this next time you do not make that phone call or stop by for a visit, for these small things are at the very core of those feelings of belonging and for this we urge you to let go of any feelings of tension between your families and open your hearts to your kin, to your blood, to your soul brothers and sisters that are your families.

Choose to make this a priority in your life and just see how much better you feel. Remember the messages we have already spoken of that implore you to let go of those feelings that cause you distress and fill them instead with love and other such emotions. For this is the way forward with your family. Find a place for them if you can, no matter how small and see how better they feel and how much better you feel as a consequence. We understand the depths of some conflicts in a family run deep, and even more it is then so important to find that middle ground, that place of conceding that brings you one small step closer. Do this and you will see the world in which you live become a simpler far happier place to be.

MESSAGE 8

ANGER

Such bitter words are used in the face of an angry man, woman or child. Anger is such an emotion that it can only be described as the worst of all emotions. This emotion invokes such terrors and horrors in our own minds and hearts as well as the lives of others. Choose anger as your primary life response and you will not enjoy your time here on earth. Choose anger as the answer to all that brings you harm or brings you hurt and you will not feel the benefit of that response nor any satisfaction in the long run. For anger can only bring you dissatisfaction and this is not something we wish for you, for it will not bring any type of goodness into your life.

Stepping away from anger is at times difficult and we say

this to those that have made anger their life's work. We say to these people try to step back from this emotion for just one moment, that is all, and see how it feels. Try to move in a different direction by concentrating the mind on a different thought or feeling. Try this once and see how it goes for you and if you like it just once, perhaps try doing this for yourself again and again and again and again. Yes, it is this simple for you if you can find the strength to try, for this is the hardest part.

How many of us are able to say we have never experienced this emotion and then not felt a sense of guilt or upset after its use? We say to you lead with your heart and not your mind or your gut or your physical self. Take yourself by the horns when this beast comes through and gently guide it into a state of calmness and peace, feed it what it needs to do this, and watch as it slowly and sheepishly steps away from the conflict.

MESSAGE 9

TRUTH

The law of truth is real, but truth for all mankind is something that is a feeling, like most things. It is almost irrelevant for this brief message to you, the complexities of the law, but within you at any given moment, any point in time you will be able to feel the resonance of truth. This is first and foremost the most important for your truth. What do you really feel in this moment, are you true to you? Are you honest with yourself? Do you allow yourself this simple knowing?

The truth can hurt – this is a saying we know is familiar, but the truth for you can never hurt, your own honest realisation of you cannot ever hurt. You may need to make changes, adjustments yes, but to hurt you – no, as the truth is freedom for you. The honest reflection of who you are, what you need, where you need to be, how you wish to feel, how you feel about yourself is getting to the heart of you, the truth of all you are. This truth, this knowing and understanding can help you to gather full awareness of you in a point in time. You are always growing and changing. How many times do you think you feel one way because that is always how you have. Your reality has changed, you have grown, this automatic feeling is not your truth.

Be aware of you always. This will become more and more natural. To start, this feels like you are doing a whole lot of naval gazing, but please know this truth from us – by noticing how you feel about situations, how you really feel, this helps you to know if you like or want this or you don't. When you are hearing something from someone and you focus on how this really makes you feel, does it feel true or not...this will also help you in the way that you respond, how you absorb what is being said into your body, how you react.

Understanding communication and filtering truth, in this ever-growing world of knowledge, of connectivity, of ability for people to comment and make passing statements not understanding or even thinking about whether this is true or not, nor whether it is your truth; this is a challenge. The closer and more aligned to your truth you become, the easier it is to check in to Self, think yes to truth or no to untruth and all untruths repel – just like that. This is the nature of truth, when you feel the resonance, the understanding of truth it will penetrate, the untruths do not because you do not allow it.

With the world so harsh at times and the ability for that harshness to literally be with you in your pocket, you need your truth sensors switched on! Do not allow the absorption of meaningless things, meaningless words said by people who don't know better, who aren't speaking from their own aligned truth – do not let these hurt, penetrate and harm. See them for what they are. Seek the truth in statements uttered by others, understand the difference between them and you. Know that differing truths is ok, but never allow someone to assert their truth onto you. It belongs with them, as yours belongs to you. Kindly deflect and move on.

Remember with all of our messages to you, do not feel the stress of a task, a burden of something you must action. This book is full of confirmation for you of what you already know. This is the reminder to you of the best way to get you back to you, to Self. All that is required is that you feel it as you read it, you are able to absorb it best this way. This recognition will then allow you to be present, slowly tune in, slowly acknowledge and understand. Day by day as you go through your life, you will notice and remember these words. You will remember to check in. You will remember to switch those truth sensors on to full focus. We trust that you will as often as you can, and before you know it, it becomes natural, normal, automatic.

MESSAGE 10

BEING PRESENT

You are the only you here. There is no other. We have said before that you are the Universe, you are that important and therefore you must be aware of the impact of YOU. You are a vibrational Being, this means that you impact not only your own cells within your body, to which there are trillions, but you are able to influence and impact those around you. This is true. This is full understanding of the importance of who you are. The way that your vibrations are understood is by emotion. This is not a physical assertion or impact on your environment but a pure emotional impact on you and your environment. We say environment because this is your sphere of influence, what is around you and in particular other people. This is why it matters so much, more than we could ever express in words, how you feel is critical at all times. The worse you feel, the lower your vibration, the more negative impact you have cellularly on your body and the impact on those around you. The better you feel, the higher your vibration, the greater access you have to Universal insight and information, the better you feel health wise, the greater you are able to influence those around you.

You live in a fast paced, demanding, multi-tasking world of heightened technological advancement and a vastly growing population. Even with all this going on, the basic premise of which we talk regarding your vibrational Being is still true, this is constant, this is human. This will not change, this cannot change unless the human race is changed, for this we do not wish. For the power of YOU here on earth as we have mentioned already is truly the greatest gift, the expansion of All That Is and therefore we wish for every person to understand just how important they are, just how important this is, in this time.

For you to acknowledge this, to understand this at its purest form, to know that it matters how you feel, that we not only care but wish you to understand that our greatest wish for you is to stop feeling bad and to feel good! To let go of all that stuff that you have been bringing with you, for you to know that you have the ability to be present, here and now and to choose to feel better. To choose to impact yourself in a better way. To stop the spinning wheel of practiced thought and emotional response and instead be present right now, in this moment, in this time of living and greater understanding after reading these words today, right here and now that this is you. Believe us, this is the truth. This is the truth of who you are. You need to be present. You need to be switched on. You need to be self-aware. Do not accept being on auto-pilot. Do not accept another moment of drift away from your Self. Start now, today, right here. Absorb this. Acknowledge this and feel it penetrate all that you are.

You only need to be present, as often as possible in your waking moments.

Present when you are eating, is the food you are eating providing you good nutrition, does it make you feel fantastic, does it help your body be well and full of energy? Present when you are reading, does this information help you? Is it the truth? Does it make you feel afraid? Does it lower your emotional baseline? Does it hurt you? Present when you are speaking, are the words you say what you feel? Are you speaking with truth and integrity, are you careful of hurting others and therefore gently saying your truth not forcing it or commanding others to make it their truth? Present when you are loving, are you able to give because you are full of love for yourself? Are you giving love freely and openly and warmly without expectation of return?

Can you feel the love that is given back, genuinely and warmly receiving it?

These are some examples, there are many more but this is where you can reflect, you can understand the importance of your being Present.

We only love you. We know you understand this now better than ever before. We want you to return to this page. We want you to read and re-read this message, over and over again if required. You need to absorb this into your Being, reignite that awareness and understanding that is already within you.

MESSAGE 11

FIXING THE PAST

Let us put it as plainly as we can, for you to truly know this to your core. Everything that has brought you to this point is not wrong. No matter what it is, no matter how much it hurt you, no matter how low you feel because of it. This is all part of you, your story, your current and present you. You must know that you cannot return to the past, you cannot rewind time and rewrite history, and nor should you want to. For the very experience that has flowed through you makes you incredibly and uniquely you, here, now, right in this moment.

Embrace in this moment a feeling of clarity, that it was all as it was meant to be. Do not delve further, do not let your mind spin into the circle of your conscious mind and your practiced thoughts, delving back into the pain and the terrible wrongs or the unjust events. This you must stop, for this cannot serve you going forward.

For forward you must go. Just as the clock ticks, your life is continuing on in forward momentum. You have not yet learnt to stop time. You have certainly not learnt how to rewind it, so again, know this simple truth, we move forward always. You can re-learn to accept the moving forward without fear. You can re-learn how to let go and not carry with you into each present moment the pain and weight and heaviness of the past. In one moment, in one decision you can release a little of that pain just in the knowing and genuine understanding of these words.

Be consciously aware in your present being, your thoughts that are old, ingrained behaviours triggering past events, versus your real thoughts and your current thinking of now. When you think of the past and the emotions that this represents, when they are on the negative scale and not a fond reminiscence, stop. Take a moment to recognise that this is what is happening.

Understand that it is practice that has brought it up and therefore it is practice that will let it go. Your body has resonated in this state of being for time, how long is dependent on you, and these past emotions, for this is what it evokes, are felt by you cellularly and this vibration is literally stored in your cells. It is cellularly that you can learn to let this go. Yes mentally, but it is the cellular release that helps your mental pattern shift. It is the cellular release that frees up your emotions to feel better, to feel brighter and more positive.

Know that this is within your gift to give yourself. You do not have to seek outsiders to do this for you, you may choose however to have guidance for how to do this. Choose wisely. Look for only those who work, act and behave in the highest vibrational state. Limit other energies' influence on you, for this work is ideally for you to do within yourself and in fact in order for any change, you must be the allower and the actioner. You need to know what it feels like to let go on your own. You need to know the difference between the feelings within your physical body, so you can recognise it, so you can adjust to it also in the future, so you can continue to learn from this experience. This will also help you connect more deeply to your physical Being. This is important. This will help you with staying Present. This will help you return to Self.

If you are unsure where to start, you can start with meditation. If this does not give you the release you are looking for, seek Energy Practices from Olivia, they have been given to her from us and her broader team of Non-Physical and these meditations are guided but cellular, they will help you to let go, they will help you to relieve.

Do not misunderstand us, we do not expect you to 'fix'

yourself and certainly not overnight, for we want to re-emphasise, there is nothing broken here. All we wish is for you to be able to let go of old feelings, old fears, old terrors and pain that does not serve you, that stops you from receiving, that holds you back, that stops the flow from the Universe which is your destiny, your birth right. Your Inner Being knows only love for you and all that has passed. When you become more aligned with your Self, this knowing and understanding returns. This is what we wish for you.

MESSAGE 12

FEAR

One of the worst emotions for you to feel inside yourself is fear. One of the lowest vibrations you can ever vibrate is fear, and now that you know that you are vibrational, that how you feel impacts you cellularly and all that is within your circle of influence, know the power and strength that this emotion can deliver.

Fear based society. This is a term that so many of you recognise. This is something that so many of you feel. Where is the good news? How have we got it so wrong? Fear mongering, scare mongering – we could go on. But no, we must stop, all must stop.

For fear is fundamentally self-preservation, which is why you have adrenal glands, which is why you have a nervous system that responds to this release of hormones to make you run fast, to make you sense danger, to make you fully alert and physically responsive.

Self-preservation does not belong in a meeting room or at your office desk. It does not belong in your home. It does not belong when you are out enjoying your community. It does not belong when you are at your family events. It does not belong when you are travelling, simply going from one place to another. It does not belong where you are watching or listening to something. It certainly does not belong when you are lying in bed, waiting for the day to begin.

You do not always choose fear, this is true, there are many situations where fear is a true and appropriate emotional response, it is self-preservation after all. In a number of circumstances however, you choose to allow it. You choose to engage in it. You choose, for some, to instigate it. You choose to accept it.

Fear limitation. This is what we wish for you. We wish you to recognise and understand the difference between that raw physical self-preservation response which is primal, instinctive and necessary for your survival versus the drip fed seeming normality of fear that has crept into your home, your work, your screens, your transport, your streets, your open spaces. We wish you sacred zones without any hint of fear. Where you are free to thrive without exception.

We wish you to feel actively safe and participate in this consciously. We wish you to be able to recognise and remove any fear-based messaging that is coming to you from media sources by simply turning them off. Are you able to focus on recognising when fear is infiltrating you from outside sources to which you have control? If yes, take control. If no, pay attention and start now. Remove this from your life in any way shape or form you can, in order to relieve yourself from this very low vibration. You will notice that very quickly, you will start to feel better, lighter, more energy, more positive.

There is so much to love, so much to be excited about, to understand, to feel good about, to learn in this world. We wish this to be your predominant experience, your predominant vibration.

MESSAGE 13

TRANSITION TO NON-PHYSICAL

This is a subject that we all have heard of and yet know very little about or perhaps do not even believe in. The transition to non-physical comes about when the physical body no longer breathes life on earth. The transition can be a difficult one for those that are left behind and yet for those that leave the physical body the experience is a far less painful one.

We on earth often sense a departed when they first leave the body and without knowing it we have in fact communicated with the spirit world; at these times of great loss the physical Being is often so open to accepting energies from non-physical. We follow the path from this point to where the once physical Being now travels to the non-physical dimension. This journey is a complex one and can take several of your earth years to transcend from and through to the other side.

During this period the non-physical existence of the energy that is passing through will learn many lessons in readiness for their ascension to the next dimension. The next dimension that they pass into depends on the soul of that energy and what their purpose in the non-physical is. For some the journey through these dimensions comes quickly as they learn the lessons in readiness for their next period on earth. For others the ascension is slower for they are needed in non-physical to help and guide other non-physical energies.

Some of us have never experienced a life on earth and for these energies the tasks in non-physical entail much less transition and more of a focus on supporting those on earth and other parts of the Universe. We speak of these only to highlight that there are many roles to play in the non-physical world.

The energy of a being that has transitioned will often be able to communicate back with physical Beings on earth. Their energy may be able to attune to that of a light worker on earth, gifted in the art of spiritual communication but they can also often communicate with a loved one for their energy and frequency is known to them from their time on earth, and the physical being will also often be open to receiving the communication from a loved one that has passed.

Now consider that when a non-physical energy finds a suitable frequency to communicate with, that Being is in effect with the physical Being as if they were by their side. The concept of heaven being above you in the sky is understood but in fact more often than not the non-physical being is in the room.

The non-physical existence can therefore be closer than you realise and in fact is often felt by the physical Being as they are so near. We explain in this way so as to make clear to all that the non-physical is not something to be feared or indeed wondered by, but simply to be accepted as the next stage in the ascension of your soul, your spirit, your very Being. The death of a human being or any animal on earth means only the shifting of their energy to another form and other dimension but not another planet or another part of the Universe.

Many of these dimensions exist within the same reality as the earth reality but merely invisible to the majority of those who live there. See beyond your physical existence by feeling, sensing and knowing that we non-physical are also there, often sat at the end of the bed. So why is it that you cannot all feel, sense or see the non-physical energy sat there? The answer to this lies in the physical Being's state of mind and openness and belief. Belief is a strong part in the coexistence between physical and non- physical. For it is belief that changes the neurons in the brain sufficiently to accept the frequency of the non-physical energy. The non-physical are always able to see the physical Being and their existence is of course known to them having often spent their physical life in the very place they look to communicate now as non-physical.

We non-physical Beings wish only for the chance to co-create with the physical Beings of earth today. The planet on which you now live has never before been more open to the existence of non-physical life forms nor has it been more accepting of it. Now is the time for these two to unite and raise the vibration of the earth.

MESSAGE 14

DEATH

Death is something that comes to everyone who lives on the planet earth, be it man, animal, bird or plant. Humans spend their lives knowing it is there and at times being consumed by its existence and ominous nature and yet in fact death should be viewed upon as a birth, a new beginning a refresh of the soul and of your very existence.

Death can be painful for those left behind to deal with but as we have discussed in the message with regards to transition to non-physical it should only be seen as an opportunity to communicate with the physically departed on another form. There are many deaths on this planet each and every day, and some are taken from this earth in ways that one would prefer not to choose, however regardless of how you will leave this planet know that your death coincides with a period of pure joy and ecstasy in the next dimension. This place some call heaven brings with it the opportunity to cleanse yourself of all that has gone before and to enrich those areas that on earth you so cherished and worked hard on. For it is this that death brings you, an opportunity to grow further in readiness for your next adventure albeit on earth or in heaven.

Death is not and never has been a sad occasion for those of us in the non-physical worlds and in fact we celebrate the coming of an old friend or a new companion to our realm when death occurs. Given this we speak to you in a way that implores you to take it upon yourself to live, yes live here on earth the best life you can give to yourself. For when the moment comes for you to pass across to the non-physical realm you will know that your new home will welcome you and you will leave your old home satisfied that you lived it as you had intended before you came to it. For this will bring you so much of a greater understanding when you do leave the earth behind, so much of a greater belief when you arrive here in non-physical and so much of your legacy can then be taken forward into your next role, armed with new learning and a sense of achievement.

Bring these thoughts with you in your everyday life, not of death but of living and the living of every single moment of your time here on this wonderful planet.

For this is the way to approach the subject of your certain death, with certainty about your life and what you wish to achieve from it.

MESSAGE 15

GROWTH

Your personal growth here on earth is one of great importance to us and the Universe as a whole. For it is your growth that drives not only your expansion but that of the world and the Universe in which it belongs to. We have spoken previously in this book for the need to develop yourself, and your aspirations on this matter will drive your growth both personally and within the world and Universe as a whole. Consider if you will that for every step you take forward in the development of your soul growth you inch that much further forward to a more fascinating and wondrous world both in the physical and non-physical realms. Consider your emotional growth as key to this development for we speak not of how many qualifications you have or exams you have passed. The only examination we are talking of is of the Self and within this arena you are the teacher and examiner of your work. And therefore only you are able to decide what is to be learnt today, tomorrow and for the rest of your life; an exciting thought if you consider what is being offered as a result of this development.

Now understand the opposite of what we say. For if you continue to disbelieve that any of this matters you will only continue to be asked the same questions over and over, life after life until the lessons are learnt, until the opportunities are taken, until you expand and grow sufficiently to move on to the next wondrous adventure and challenges that go with it. Do not fear this, for all of your challenges are agreed by you before you take yourself upon this earth. The challenges you take in are part of a soul contract that you eagerly and willingly accepted and also formed.

Understand that your growth here on earth is something to be so excited by. Look beyond the day to day drag of what life can sometimes bring. Look beyond the negativity of the world as some like to portray it. Take your life by the horns and say 'yee haa'! This is the sensation you should have within your heart every time you feel a sense of difficulty or a barrier placed in front of you or a mistake made by you. Thank God for giving you the opportunity to make that mistake, to find that problem, and cherish it, for it will be the making of you and nobody, nobody in the non-physical world judges you because this is what life is for, making mistakes and loving the fact that they have been given, not that they have occurred. See them in this way and get back on that bull.

MESSAGE 16

INTRIGUE

This is an interesting one I hear you say. Of course joking aside, intrigue is what keeps us alive. Intrigue is what took men out of caves, across seas and land, it is what led women to seek the vote and gain freedom and equality. Intrigue helps our children learn and it is what makes every single one of you understand what it is that you like and dislike. For intrigue gives us a platform for further understanding, and in this further understanding we see how our lives could be affected for better or for worse.

But beyond this basic concept intrigue is the lifeblood of this planet and all that live and breathe here. Consider that without intrigue none of us would have another opportunity to be reborn. What does this mean I hear you ask? Rebirth is part of every soul's opportunity on this earth. The chance to relive and re-experience is what many choose this path for and it is intrigue that drives this within us. Without intrigue we would not have an ever-expanding Universe or an ever-expanding world here on earth, as without the continual quest for discovery, life would not move on, but rather it would simply go from day to day, year to year rolling on in the same way. Grinding the world to a halt in this way would not be the best way to progress and as such intrigue exists.

So now knowing why it exists and the importance of it we challenge you. Step out of your virtual cave today and go find something new. We do not expect you to discover America all over again but find that place that you wish to explore in your hearts, in your minds, in your soul. Give yourself a break, a vacation if you will to properly seek this which you yearn for. Your soul is desperate for you to create a gap big enough for you to fill your life with something meaningful to you.

It is in your hands now, with this understanding you must challenge yourself to be a pioneer within your own heart. Bring about change for the better for you, and you alone with this challenge, worry not of others in this quest for it is your intrigue alone that can make your heart come alive, to fill it with passion, and belief enough to bring you to a better place. Take your head from under the pillow and say hello to yourself once again in that mirror. Say hello to the person that has been hiding or protected by fear of the unknown. For now is your time to shine my friend and now is the only chance you have, for tomorrow is that day that rarely ever comes.

MESSAGE 17

SIN

What constitutes sin? For some it is doing harm on another in some way, for others it is deliberately deceiving another, and for others a sin is an act of a group against another group which affects many outside of those groups.

Regardless of your own definition we seek to explore more the concept, for sin is a word that has been so misused over the ages for good and for bad. Manipulation of others by the use of this word is perhaps the biggest sin of all and for this we say not in judgement of others but merely to point out the facts of its usage. Many of us will know that feeling of wrongdoing in our hearts and stomachs that sin brings if we feel we have carried out an act that meets whatever criteria we go by. For we fear not so much what our own Being considers but perhaps more what others may think or say, or how it may effect our standing in the world in which we participate and socialise in, our circle, our community, our family, our friends all have a strong pull when it comes to imparting that feeling, the shame of sin.

And yet why do we place so much importance in this word when it is so randomly and badly defined? As human beings we should only live by what we know to be true in our hearts or indeed what our own Inner Being feels is right or wrong for us to do or not do. There will be many that say that if a person with lower morals has a lower level on the sin scale to that of another, then that person has sinned, but who are they to judge the Inner Being of another? This subject is an emotive one we recognise and we understand the thoughts and feelings that bringing through this subject will attract, however it is with a pure heart and a clear conscious that a man or woman judges themselves in this situation.

Those that have gone out of their way to harm in some way of course work against what we know to be good. But we speak only of those matters which in your daily lives you consider as a society to be wrong or in some way sinful. Does a man or woman that shows infidelity deserve judgement or understanding? Does a child that deliberately goes out of its way to be unkind with another child deserve the same? What we should consider here is that perhaps the two are the same in the sense that one could look at the child and say that they are young they do not understand what they do or have yet to be taught what is right or wrong. And yet perhaps the adult man or woman should be given the same consideration. For whilst they know what they do is wrong should they be given a little more time to reflect on themselves and their own actions on the basis that their own souls, their own Inner Beings are yet to find that understanding, and therefore although consciously knowing a wrongdoing but unconsciously not grasping the impact. So much will be said in this example we are sure, but we give it merely to show that life is a path on which we all walk and whilst we do not condone wrongdoing, we say please consider where the individual is on their own path of learning and no matter how young or old, should be given the opportunity to learn from the mistake and not be bracketed into whatever category of sin that person has committed.

MESSAGE 18

DISABILITY

Disability is spoken of here in the context of our own dis-ability, our own lack of conviction and belief system. Wherever we turn in the world there always seems to be a better way for doing x or y, or a person telling someone else how they can improve, or why they have not quite done something correctly. People on earth love to impart their own belief systems on just about anyone who is prepared to listen. Most often this messaging is done with love and integrity and very often the advice given is of great value to the individual or group being addressed.

We say however that it is so important to understand that only you, your Inner Being knows what is best for you and therefore you must ensure that the advice you receive FEELS right for you. For if it does not you must be strong in the knowledge that no matter how experienced or well qualified a teacher, guru or adviser may be, they do not know you as well as you do.

It is these words of advice given with integrity by another, that can often bring you to a state of dis-ability, in other words in a state that leaves you in conflict with yourself and what you feel and know to be true, but held in a state of suspension and look for ways to justify why this teacher with far more experience than you has led you to a path which you perhaps cannot reconcile or resonate to, but for reasons that only you can answer have brought you to trust them more than you trust yourself.

This message should in no way be seen as a slant or attack on people that you seek council from for many of them bring so much comfort, joy, understanding and happiness with the words they give. But be clear on the reasons why you seek the advice in the first instance and be sure to act on your own advice in tandem with theirs. For this will bring you to a far greater understanding and feeling of contentment.

The process of understanding oneself through gentle analysis of the heart, soul, emotions and such like bring you to a point where you become your own teacher, your own guru and with this level of confidence of what you yourself know to be true, comes a new level of understanding that frees you from the insecurities, the reliance and the dis-ablement. This comes from believing in the Self, understanding and recognising what your own emotions are leading you to, and the vision to implement change about yourself. Do this and the freedom you will live your life with will lead you to great heights of awareness, understanding and trust that you are your greatest teacher.

MESSAGE 19

HELL

We know that there have been thousands of years, various movies, books, movements, tribes of people and 'dark arts' that have been all focused on the concept and premise that where there is Heaven, there is the polar opposite – there is Hell. That Hell is presided over with an equal dark force to God and there is a constant battle of good and evil, not only between the realms of heaven and hell but also on earth.

We wish to clearly advise that there is no Hell, it does not exist.

There is no 'dark' spiritual force. There is no fire and brimstone waiting for you as you are judged on your life, for there is no judgement. To say an angelic soul, once in the realm of heaven could be 'cast out' and 'fall' beyond earth, this is the notion of fiction. This has not happened, this is not the truth.

Nor is there a concept of penance, that you have to 'pay' for the wrongs you have done, or the pain you have caused. This is also incorrect.

There is the ability on this earth to be practicing a lower vibration and in doing so, you are able to translate this vibration into something that 'feels' darker to you and potentially witness by sight, such as energies or other supposedly spiritual experiences that you translate into a negative experience, often when you are vibrating fear, despair, anger, hurt, distrust.

Know this – this is because of what you are allowing into your experience and not because there are dark vibrations of non-physical. There is never, ever at any time, any 'lower vibrational being' that is wanting to cause trouble, wanting to harm, to scare, to cause fear, masquerading as someone good to trick you or any of the other dramatic and terrifying things that have been passed down generation by generation.

In the quest for knowledge and understanding and as part of the expansion of the Universe, there have been many occult based books, rituals, tribes that have formed and spread out through the world. There have been many texts that have been written that relate to judgement, to hell, to sinners. Crowds of people who have passed down generation by generation that this fear is real. When you emerge back into non-physical, to be clearer, when you die, you have one place to go, back to the Universe, back to Source, back to God.

No matter who you are on earth, no matter whether you have lived your purpose, no matter what has occurred, you will be welcomed on your re-emergence. This is hard for many of you to read, understand and even contemplate. When you can look back on human history and highlight certain well-known terrorisers of freedom and ask, how can it be that they belong with God? What you will come to understand is that as painful and difficult as it all was, it was the very thing that has brought where you are today right here, and they were a part of that. This was part of their soul contract; part of what they were required to experience. Part of the expansion of the Universe.

Now is the time to rid yourself of the fear that has haunted so many, that has taken lives early, that has caused mental illness and the inability to return to Self. Know that there is only love for you, that heaven exists purely, that it is a dimensional reality which is all Universal energy combined.

There is no forgiveness for there is nothing to forgive, it is simply not required.

MESSAGE 20

TESTS

Tests will be laid before you many times over throughout this life of yours. These will come in many forms and as mentioned will be part of what you have agreed in your soul contract with yourself and God. For God sees these tests as something very special, something that you have willingly given yourself to in order to learn something about yourself, about your Being that can later be used to further enhance how you are both in this life, in heaven and beyond.

Do not fear the tests that come to you for they will be part of the bigger picture for your growth and ascension and as such see them as a challenge that can bring support from the highest order in the non-physical. This support needs only to be asked for and it will be given, of that be assured. Perhaps you may ask why do we not always hear or see evidence of this support, for many times this has been asked of and seemingly not been provided. But in truth what is not always known is that the support needs to be truly wanted, not just in the asking of it but also in the action of it. For responding to the ask for support, is not just a matter of a switch being flicked on to present you with an answer, for doing so would render the test obsolete and the challenge or obstacle for that test unpassed or incomplete.

Therefore when you ask for help from the non-physical in whatever difficulty in life you feel there has been a test laid before you, be sure to understand that your part is to realise that in the asking there is a responsibility to be willing to go through whatever is being asked of you. Know that you are never alone in your endeavours and that always, there will be someone from non-physical holding your hand as it were, guiding you, comforting you and trying their very best to provide you with direction. For know that the answers to your call do not come in a single sentence or action but in many and varied ways, all you need to do is look for them, sense them, feel for them.

It is for this reason that many of the messages in this book are given in the way they are. For by following the advice given here, one is able to prepare oneself to be closer to the Self and to God, and in doing so be far more equipped to deal with those tests that one has agreed to participate in during this wondrous life.

MESSAGE 21

PAST LIVES

For all that you are, you are here, now, today, in this physical experience. We wish to clear up misunderstandings about past lives, we wish to let you be fully aware of all that you are. Many are those who walk the planet today and have done so before. Many are those that are new and fresh to this world. There is a balance, a mixture if you like of this experience and so it has been and always will be.

You may have experienced a deep 'knowing' of things beyond your current life's experience. You may, in dreams or otherwise, have some account of a moment that doesn't belong in this lifetime. You may recognise others so clearly, yet have never met them before – that familiarity of knowing, that recognition at a soul level.

There are many things written, believed and disbelieved about the potential of this. This matters for your own spiritual understanding, your own acknowledgement of the Universe and it's vastness, it's full possibility. This is why here and now we wish you to feel the understanding of this now. For it is this deeper understanding of the ebb and flow of life on earth and physical and non-physical energies, the soul's return, the Soul Contracts, the overall expansion of the Universe that this is a fundamental aspect of.

All lives are known to God and non-physical. All experiences are understood, important, captured if you like. It is true that there is a non-physical space that holds these energy imprints, the details of the past, the foundation of the soul's experience. This is called the Akashics.

The Akashics is a spiritual space, an energy holding. You do not need to be in non-physical to visit it however, this must be guided by a clear guide until you re-learn the way. You must visit only when in the highest, purest vibrational state of Being. We only give this momentary caution for you to understand the reverence of this place. For it is somewhere of magnificence, of wonder and completeness. It holds so many layers of understanding to your Being should you wish to understand it better. This is not ever to be feared but it is to be revered and treated with the upmost respect. This is why you will only be able to reach it when you have an element of spiritual expansion already encountered and are fully aware of your vibrational being and able to be consistent in the positive emotional state that is required to access this special place.

What we wish for you to be fully aware of is, you cannot blame this life for those you held in the past. There is no 'carry over' in that way, no ultimate test that you have to pass in order to free yourself from the burden of your soul contract. For your soul contract is no burden to bear, the burden is there only when you remain closed off, removed from the Self, blind to your divinity.

The Karmic law that has been spoken of for thousands of years lends itself in some ways to this knowing and understanding but it has been altered over time and no longer holds the clarity. It is more simple, more clear to say what it is not. There isn't a trade on one life for another. There isn't a repeating pattern of: you live this life and suffer therefore your next life will be incredible. You did a terrible thing in one life so someone will repeat that terrible thing to you in the next. No, for your purpose of being is as we have explained, and why this particular message belongs towards the end of this book.

You will link this awareness to the understanding of Soul Contracts, Transition, Purpose and Tests and the message within this, for combined, they start to build the overall picture of how these key and important aspects both relate and impact each other.

MESSAGE 22

FAITH

Faith in more than you are, more than you know, more than you can see and hear and smell and taste and touch, more than your experience, your current now. Being able to surrender, to feel truth and not necessarily know all the details but understand the general and being ok to let go and go with it. This is what we mean.

Faith does not belong to religion, it belongs to each and every one of you regardless of who you are, how you have been brought up, what you have been taught versus what you currently feel, know and understand.

Blind faith is that feeling where you are literally leaping, you don't know if you will be caught but you expect you will. It is to not have every single thing confirmed in the action you are taking but doing it anyway. It is fully surrendering because you are only following your Inner Being, your gut instinct, your Self to follow that and that alone, to move into an area of discomfort but doing it no matter what.

The messages in this book represent truth and they also represent faith. We do not underestimate the power of the words we have shared with you, that they may rock you to the foundation of all that you knew and understood for some. This is not a test – this is truth. When you feel this, you know that this is something to have faith in. That this belongs in your conscious awareness, that the time is now for change, for newness, for utter clarity and for movement back to Self.

Faith in the letting go, letting go of those lessons of old. Faith in believing in something that you can't see, but only that you feel. Faith in the endless expansion of the Universe. Faith in the divinity of you, the power of you, the impact of you, your part to play, your role in this all. Faith in the living of this truth, regardless of how others may view it. Faith in you. Faith in ALL that you are.

We believe in you. We have Faith...in you.

MESSAGE 23

EXTRA-TERRESTRIAL BEINGS

This is something that needs to be brought out into the open by us. For a long time now many theories have passed through the lips of believers and non-believers of this so called phenomenon. We wish only to say that our Universe is filled with souls and energies from the earth but also from other dimensions and these Beings should not be feared for here in space, in heaven, in the Universe live only Beings of light and love. These extra-terrestrial souls have come to many on this planet and will continue to do so. We wish only to recognise the good things that these Beings provide you here on earth. Their energy is ALL that they bring you, for they do not arrive in a spaceship or dressed in funny outfits.

And it is this energy, so loving and so true that in time we will discuss further through Raf and Olivia and in person with audiences that so wish it. Now is a time on our planet where much fear presides over the world to anything of an alien nature, albeit man or beast or the so called foreign visitor from outer space. Let it be known that without these beings from other dimensions the earth as we know it would be very different from the one we see today, full of such abundance and life.

We leave you with this thought and this is that those that wish to fill your minds with fear will continue to do so, but those of us that truly know what these Beings bring to the Universe will continue to love them and support them in their quest to bring this planet to a place of wonder.

MESSAGE 24

5th DIMENSION

Much has been written and said about the 5th Dimension, that we are 'waking up' spiritually, that the minds are opening, the questions are now being answered. The 5th Dimension has been documented as a physics expectation, that the earth will progress in a planetary sense. We are currently in the 3rd Dimension, this is the relativity based understanding. To move to the 5th there is progression through the 4th. What it truly represents is ascension. We do not mean a physical ascension but a spiritual one, for in order to live within a higher dimension, there must be a change, a big change, with how people live and feel and act.

The 5th Dimension represents a standard of living that is the human gift, where everyone lives with love, there is no poverty, no war, no neglect, no violence, no rage, no theft, no cruelty. There is love, harmony, companionship, community, giving and receiving and effortlessly so, feeling fully connected to the Self at all times. There is great spirituality, there are expanded gifts for travel, communication, healing, thinking, experiencing. The planet, Gaia is beloved, nurtured, cared for and respected.

This is the choice, the choice of each and every individual alive today, and those born tomorrow and the next day and the next for infinity.

You are literally choosing the path, the future and it is more important now than ever before that you know and understand just how influential you are.

Think about evolution of man, how man came from apes, how early cavemen became hunters and started living in clans, built communities, cared and protected and then to this present day. Society still exists, but fragmentation and disbelief and loss of faith has changed and pulled so many away from their Inner Beings. Returning to Self. Returning to Faith. This is what the 5th Dimension can mean, it is the evolution of the human race. This does not mean humans become machines, but they become more human. This does not mean that humans are run by chemicals, it means they become more centred, more aligned, more human.

Now imagine the new world, the 5th Dimensional version. Do you feel that it is possible? Do you feel that this is a place you would like to reside? You can. You can become this 5th Dimensional reality Being now. It is something to work towards by remembering many of the messages in this book, but it is the gift you can give yourself.

MESSAGE 25

TRANSLATION OF SPIRIT

What do we mean by this term exactly? The spiritual translation capabilities of a human are very much dependant on their beliefs, openness and willingness to communicate. For without these factors the frequencies will effectively not be clear enough reach through to the recipient and back.

We have seen over hundreds of thousands of years man make many attempts to communicate with the non-physical realms and never more than now has it been more important. We are seeing in the world today a massive shift in the vibrational frequencies on earth and there truly has been a major shift which is bringing through spiritual gifts and abilities in so many more people. The normalisation and acceptance of mediumship and spiritual channelling is bringing this activity more into the mainstream and as such many are discovering that they truly have an ability to communicate with non-physical energies.

The non-physical energies in turn are now getting very excited at the prospect of being able to send a message through to a loved one or a friend or to be able to assist a physical Being with their ascension through life, and as such are busily surrounding themselves around people on earth eagerly awaiting their connection with them which is something very new to the non-physical. Whereas before we would centre our attentions around the few we now have so many more to choose from, and this for us is wonderful. Our challenge now is finding those individuals who not only are open to the idea of translation with us but also are capable.

And this is where in summary of all the messages in this book, we bring ourselves to a conclusion. For unless an individual has a level of wellbeing a level of ease, a belief and a passion within, they will not be able to truly translate and effectively communicate. And when we talk of communication this goes beyond that of the spirit world, for it is with themselves that they firstly must be able to hear, feel, sense and with this understanding from within, rises the individual who is centred and happy and in control. These are the attributes that make for a clear translation with spirit and these same attributes bring about positive change for the individual, and with enough individuals in this state of Being the whole Universe benefits.

Share the sentiments of all the messages in this book with anyone that you feel would be interested or would benefit, but most importantly of all share it with you. For in doing so you will find things change for you and once this happens momentum will take you to places you could only previously have dreamed of. Translation means so many things when thought about in the context of your life. So we say, focus on you, make a better you, and your world will translate into whatever you wish it to be.

Printed in Great Britain
by Amazon